Ripley's Believe It or Not!

Developed and produced by Ripley Publishing Ltd

This edition published and distributed by:

Mason Crest
450 Parkway Drive, Suite D, Broomall, PA 19008
www.masoncrest.com

Printed and bound in the United States of America

First printing
9 8 7 6 5 4 3 2 1

Ripley's Believe It or Not!
Eccentric Tales
ISBN: 978-1-4222-2777-0 (hardback)
ISBN: 978-1-4222-2794-7 (paperback)
ISBN: 978-1-4222-9038-5 (e-book)
Ripley's Believe It or Not!—Complete 8 Title Series
ISBN: 978-1-4222-2769-5

Cataloging-in-Publication Data on file with the Library of Congress

PUBLISHER'S NOTE
While every effort has been made to verify the accuracy of the entries in this book, the
Publisher's cannot be held responsible for any errors contained in the work. They would
be glad to receive any information from readers.

WARNING
Some of the stunts and activities in this book are undertaken by experts and should not
be attempted by anyone without adequate training and supervision.

Ripley's Believe It or Not!®

Enter If You Dare

ECCENTRIC TALES

www.MasonCrest.com

ECCENTRIC TALES

Strange but true. Open up
and find extraordinary stories,
astounding animals, and impressive
feats. Read about gruesome parasites,
the giant-sized turban, and the
frog that swallowed a lightbulb!

This yucky parasite replaces the tongue of a
fish, and feeds on blood and mucus...

LAVA JUNKY

PATRICK KOSTER WILL DO ANYTHING TO GET A GOOD PICTURE—EVEN SLEEP ON THE EDGE OF AN ACTIVE VOLCANO! THE DUTCH ENGINEER BEGAN PHOTOGRAPHING NATURAL PHENOMENA OVER TEN YEARS AGO. HE BECAME OBSESSED WITH CAPTURING THE VIOLENT POWER OF VOLCANOES, CALLING HIMSELF A "LAVA JUNKY," AND EVEN PROPOSING TO HIS WIFE NEXT TO A SIMMERING CRATER.

TO GET THE BEST SHOTS, KOSTER RISKS INHALING TOXIC GAS, SUFFOCATION FROM HOT ASH, AND LETHAL VOLCANIC BOMBS— LUMPS OF MOLTEN ROCK VIOLENTLY EJECTED FROM ERUPTING VOLCANOES—NOT TO MENTION THE UNSTOPPABLE FLOW OF SUPER- HOT LAVA SURGING PAST HIS CAMERA. DESPITE THE DANGERS, KOSTER WEARS REGULAR CLOTHING, WITH ONLY A GAS MASK FOR PROTECTION FROM NOXIOUS GAS. HE HAS PHOTOGRAPHED VOLCANOES ON THE CANARY ISLANDS, AND IN ETHIOPIA, ITALY, GREECE, AND HAWAII AMONG OTHERS, AND HAS A LONG LIST OF OTHER LAVA-SPEWING CRATERS HE INTENDS TO VISIT.

At this burning lava lake in the crater of active volcano Erta Ale, the surface is constantly moving and bubbling, spewing potentially lethal sulphur dioxide gas. The surrounding terrain is rough and crumbling, meaning Patrick has to watch his footing very carefully to avoid falling into the lava lake.

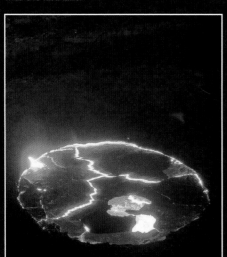

Lava from Kilauea pouring into Pacific Ocean, Big Island, Hawaii. The lava can explode on contact with the sea, throwing lava unpredictably into the air. Another danger here is the appearance of plumes of toxic gas, which contain hydrochloric acid, volcanic ash, and needle-sharp lava pieces.

Colorful salt flats, Dallol, Ethiopia. The earth's crust is very thin here, resulting in striking volcanic features when very hot salt water rises to the surface. The area is extremely hot; temperatures can reach over 140°F (60°C) so dehydration is a real risk.

Patrick standing on the edge of a lava fountain on the most active volcano on earth, Kilauea, Big Island, Hawaii. The molten lava here is over 2,012°F (1,100°C).

RIPLEY'S *ask*

There are many different places to photograph, why volcanoes in particular?
After putting in a lot of effort each time, I hope to witness one of nature's most destructive forces, capture its beauty, and walk away from it safely with a lot of pictures. There are only a handful of people doing this kind of photography worldwide. In my country, The Netherlands, I am the only one. Experiencing a real volcanic eruption for the first time is unbelievable. It is all about the smell of sulfur, the sound like a jet engine, the explosions like bombs going off, ash and stones falling down, poor visibility. The feeling of adrenaline combined with fear while taking photographs is addictive. You just want more.

How hot does it get?
Lava can get extremely hot. A sudden lava fountain in the Erta Ale pit crater generated so much extra heat that I fled the crater's edge afraid that my clothes would catch fire.

What is the worst aspect of photographing volcanoes?
The extreme conditions. Cameras, tripods, and lenses have all failed because of volcanic ash and gases. There is also the risk of being hurt while hiking up a volcano's summit or through lava fields, and the worst form of altitude sickness is also a problem. There is danger from inhaling toxic gas or volcanic ash, or being hit by lava bombs during an explosion.

What is the best aspect?
After the extreme effort of getting to the volcano's crater, actually experiencing— seeing, hearing, feeling, smelling— something unique.

Do you ever get scared?
Yes and it's a good thing. You stay alert and sharp to react immediately if something extraordinary happens. It also makes you more careful. The best picture is not necessarily the one taken closest to the action.

Have you ever been caught out?
I have had some narrow escapes. In Tanzania a small lava "bridge" collapsed in the boiling lava pit moments after I left. In Hawaii I stood on edges that were gone the next day (called bench collapse). They had fallen into the ocean. The seawater is extremely hot at these places so survival is almost impossible. Another time on Stromboli the conditions at the summit were so poor, with wind blowing ash and toxic gases right over the summit, that a gas mask and helmet needed to be used. Taking pictures was not an option under those conditions.

Silk Cocoon

A motorist returned to his car in Rotterdam, the Netherlands, in 2009 to find it buried beneath a giant silk cocoon created by an army of caterpillars. His Honda car had somehow been mistaken for food by spindle ermine larvae, which weave silk webs to protect themselves from birds and wasps, allowing them to gorge on leaves for six weeks before transforming into butterflies.

ℝ BIRD LOVER

A male traveler arriving at Los Angeles International Airport, California, in 2009 was found to have 14 live birds strapped to his legs under his pants. Customs officials became suspicious after spotting bird feathers and droppings on his socks, and tail feathers protruding beneath his pants.

ℝ HIDING PLACE

Two-year-old Natalie Jasmer from Greenville, Pennsylvania, did such a good job of hiding during a 2009 game of hide-and-seek that her family had to call police and firefighters to help find her. After an hour's search, she was finally found by the family dog, having fallen asleep in a drawer beneath the washing machine.

ℝ INSEPARABLE TWINS

Identical twins Peter and Paul Kingston from West Sussex, England, have been almost inseparable for over 75 years. They worked for the same electronics firm and then as entertainers at the same holiday camp, and for the past 40 years they have shared the same house with their respective wives.

ℝ BOXED CLEVER

A prisoner escaped jail in Willich, Germany, in November 2008 by hiding in a box, which was part of a courier's shipment.

ℝ ID PROBLEM

A judge presiding over a drug trafficking case in Kuala Lumpur, Malaysia, released the defendants—identical twins—because police officers couldn't prove which one had originally been arrested.

ℝ GRAVE DISCOVERY

In March 2009, while planting bushes, Sheila Woods of Devon, England, uncovered a grave, complete with headstone, coffin, and corpse from 1833, in the middle of her garden.

Scissor Spider

Security guards at American airports confiscate hundreds of scissors and other potential weapons every day. Artist Christopher Locke collects these spiky tools and bends them into sculptures, including spiders made from twisted scissors and creepy crawlies made from knives and multi-tools.

ℝ STRAY BULLET

In July 2009, Janifer Bliss was accidentally shot while sitting on the toilet, when the person in the next-door cubicle dropped their gun and it went off. Bliss was sitting in the cubicle in a hotel bathroom in Tampa, Florida, when she was hit in the leg by the stray bullet, which was fired as the handgun fell to the ground.

ℝ BABY SWITCH

Kay Rene Reed Qualls and DeeAnn Angell Shafer learned at the age of 56 that they had been accidentally switched at birth and had grown up with each other's parents. The girls were born at Pioneer Memorial Hospital in Heppner, Oregon, in 1953, but the mistake was only uncovered when they took DNA tests in 2009.

℞ BEETLE TERROR

In December 2008, police in Osaka, Japan, arrested a man for releasing thousands of beetle larvae onto an express train to scare female passengers.

℞ SWALLOWED PHONE

When Andrew Cheatle lost his cell phone on a beach at Worthing, West Sussex, England, he thought it had been swept out to sea and that he would never see it again, but a week later it turned up—in the belly of a huge cod. The 25-lb (11-kg) cod had been caught by fisherman Glen Kerley, who was gutting it for his fish stall when he found the phone—which still worked—inside the fish's stomach.

℞ LEAP DAY

The Keogh family have three generations born on 29 February, beating odds of 3,118,535,181 to one. Peter Keogh was born in Ireland on leap day—February 29—1940, his son Eric was born in the U.K. on leap day 1964, and granddaughter Bethany was born in the U.K. on leap day 1996.

℞ WILD CHILD

A Russian girl spent the first five years of her life being brought up by cats and dogs. The girl, from the Siberian city of Chita, adopted the behavior of the animals she lived with, even barking like a little dog and jumping at the door when people left the room.

℞ CLOSE RELATIVES

After not seeing each other for 60 years, long-lost siblings George Culwick and Lucy Heenan discovered in 2008 that they had been living just 4 mi (6.5 km) apart in Birmingham, West Midlands, England.

℞ CLOUD NINE

To mark the ninth day of the ninth month of 2009, a budget supermarket chain in Los Angeles, California, offered nine couples cut-rate wedding ceremonies for 99 cents. After getting hitched, the couples were handed $99.99 in cash and taken to a romantic location for their honeymoon.

℞ CASH CATCH

Two Australian teenagers who went on a fishing trip to Tuntable Creek, near Nimbin, New South Wales, in September 2009 landed a surprise catch—a plastic package containing $87,000 in cash.

TRAVELING TWINS

CHANG AND ENG BUNKER (1811–74) WERE THE ORIGINAL SIAMESE TWINS, THE RARE CONDITION BEING NAMED AFTER THEIR BIRTHPLACE OF SIAM (MODERN-DAY THAILAND). THEY WERE JOINED AT THE STOMACH BY A SMALL PIECE OF CARTILAGE AND WERE LATER EXHIBITED AS A CURIOSITY. THEY WENT ON TO MARRY TWO SISTERS AND HAD A TOTAL OF 21 CHILDREN. IN 1874, CHANG SUFFERED A STROKE IN HIS SLEEP AND WHEN ENG AWOKE TO FIND HIS BROTHER DEAD, HE REFUSED TO BE SEPARATED FROM HIM AND BLED TO DEATH THREE HOURS LATER, BECAUSE THE BLOOD WAS NOT BEING PUMPED BACK FROM HIS TWIN'S BODY.

JULY

Past pheasant given up the ghost on the Warwick Highway.

		SAT	17
		SUN	18
THU	1	MON	19
FRI	2	TUE	20
SAT	3	WED	21
SUN	4	THU	22
MON	5	FRI	23
TUE	6	SAT	24
WED	7	SUN	25
THU	8	MON	26
FRI	9	TUE	27
SAT	10	WED	28
SUN	11	THU	29
MON	12	FRI	30
TUE	13	SAT	31
WED	14		
THU	15		
FRI	16		

ROADKILL CALENDAR

KEVIN BERESFORD TRAVELED ALL OVER BRITAIN TAKING PHOTOGRAPHS OF ROADKILL FOR A 2010 CALENDAR THAT BECAME A BEST-SELLER. HE SOLD HUNDREDS OF COPIES OF HIS QUIRKY ROADKILL CALENDAR, WHICH FEATURED PICTURES OF SQUASHED SQUIRRELS, FLATTENED FOXES, AND MASHED MAGPIES.

ROAD KILL

CALENDAR 2010

No animal was deliberately killed or maimed in the production of this calendar

℞ MOON CHECK

A $10.50 check signed by Neil Armstrong hours before he took off for the Moon was sold for $27,350 at an auction in Amherst, New Hampshire, in July 2009—40 years to the day after it was written. Armstrong had written the check—for money borrowed from a NASA manager—in case anything happened to him on the lunar mission.

℞ DENTAL DISCOVERY

A customer shopping at a Walmart store in Falmouth, Massachusetts, said he found ten human teeth hidden in a zipped compartment of a wallet he was about to buy. Police said the teeth belonged to an adult, but since there was no blood or gum tissue present, it would not be possible to perform DNA tests to identify whose teeth they were.

℞ DELAYED DELIVERY

Dave Conn of Hudson, Ohio, received a postcard in his mailbox 47 years after it was sent. The card had been sent by a woman from Helena, Montana, in 1962, but the delay meant it never reached its intended recipient, who had died in 1988.

℞ BOTTLE VOYAGE

A bottle with a note inside thrown into the ocean in 1969 off the coast of New Jersey was discovered 39 years later—just 400 mi (645 km) away in Corolla, North Carolina.

℞ FREE SALAMI

Motorists in the Bulgarian capital Sofia were awarded free salami in 2009 for driving courteously. As part of a police road-safety initiative, a salami factory offered lunch to any driver who yielded to pedestrians at marked street crossings.

℞ DOUBLE MONEY

In August 2009, customers flocked to a faulty cash machine that was paying out double money at a store in London, England. The store closed the machine as soon as it learned of the fault, but by then lucky customers had taken over $7,500 from it.

® ROWERS' RESCUE

The pilot of a light aircraft forced to bale out in the middle of the Irish Sea had a lucky escape when he was spotted by a team trying to row its way around Britain. The four-man crew was ten days into its time challenge when one of them saw the plane half-submerged in the freezing water. Pilot John O'Shaughnessy, who had been flying from Wales to Ireland, was standing on the wing.

® INCRIMINATING EVIDENCE

Vlado Taneski, a Macedonian crime reporter, covered a series of murders in such detail that police eventually discovered in June 2008 that he was responsible for them!

® GREENBRIER GHOST

A ghost once helped convict a murderer. Zona Shue's death in Greenbrier County, West Virginia, in 1897 was presumed natural until her spirit appeared to her mother and described how she was killed by her husband Edward. Her mother persuaded the local prosecutor to reopen the case and an autopsy on the exhumed body verified that Zona had been murdered. Edward was subsequently convicted of the crime.

® UNWANTED CUSTOMERS

Shoppers at a food store in Puyallup, Washington State, were forced to flee in 2009 after cattle broke away from a fair parade and ran amok in the aisles. A year earlier, in 2008, a bull from the same fair charged into a bank.

® BAR BLAZE

In 2008, a fire crew from the town of Bournemouth in Dorset, England, was sent to extinguish a blaze at a bar called The Inferno—which was situated next to another bar called The Old Fire Station.

® CORK ATTACK

After a truck carrying bottles of wine crashed and caught fire on a highway in Wamsutter, Wyoming, emergency crews came under attack from a hail of corks as the bottles exploded in the heat.

® BANK ERROR

Josh Muszynski of Manchester, New Hampshire, swiped his debit card at a gas station to pay for a pack of cigarettes in July 2009. He then checked his account online and saw that he had been charged over $23 quadrillion. The Bank of America corrected the error the following day.

Car Crazy

After spending 17 years building his own Lamborghini sports car in the cellar of his Wisconsin home, Ken Imhoff realized that he had no way of getting it out. Undeterred, he built a ramp and hired a mechanical digger to gouge out a slope in his garden, even removing a section of the house's foundations. At the end of a delicate 2½-hour operation, the new car finally emerged above ground.

® FAMILY LINE

After six generations spanning 217 years, the last Dr. Maurice of the town of Marlborough in Wiltshire, England, finally hung up his stethoscope in 2009. Dr. David Maurice's retirement brought to an end an unbroken line of family members caring for the town's sick people dating back to 1792.

® BODY HOAX

Police officers received a tip-off about what appeared to be a body wrapped in a sleeping bag in a forest near Izu City, Japan. They took it back to the station for a post-mortem examination—but when the medical examiner opened the bag, he found it contained a life-size doll wearing a brown wig, a blouse, and a skirt.

® BUCKET CEREMONY

In keeping with a tradition in Xi'an, China, that the bride's feet should not touch the ground during the journey from home to the ceremony, a couple got married in 2008 in midair in two large tractor digger buckets. The bride and two bridesmaids stood in one bucket, while the groom and two best men stood opposite them in a second bucket.

Something Fishy

An unidentified 4½-ft-long (1.4-m) fish caught near Taizhou City in eastern China, had a large sucker pad on its head. No villager would eat the weird-looking creature in case its appearance was the result of toxic poisoning.

℞ LATE DEMAND

A German mathematician, who had been dead for 450 years, received a letter in 2009 demanding that he pay long-overdue TV licence fees. The bill was sent to the last home address of algebra expert Adam Ries, even though he had died in 1559—centuries before the invention of television.

℞ GRATEFUL THIEF

An Italian thief thanked police for rescuing him from a group of irate Korean tourists whom he had just robbed. The thief had stolen a handbag from the family during their visit to Rome, but they gave chase and floored him with taekwondo moves, before subjecting him to a beating. They stopped only when an officer arrived to arrest the 48-year-old man.

℞ DOLPHIN GAMES

A woman who had been playing with a friendly bottlenose dolphin called Moko in the sea off Mahia Beach on New Zealand's North Island got into difficulty when the dolphin stopped her from returning to shore. Her cries for help eventually alerted rescuers who rowed out to find her exhausted and cold, clinging to a buoy. Locals say the dolphin gets lonely in the winter when there are fewer people around and just wanted to keep playing.

℞ CUCUMBER THEFTS

In 2009, police in Adelaide, Australia, investigated a series of thefts involving cucumbers. More than $8,500 worth of cucumbers were stolen in 11 separate burglaries on market gardens over a period of three months.

℞ LOTTERY LUCK

In 2002, Mike McDermott from Hampshire, England, won the lottery twice with the same numbers, beating odds of 5.4 trillion to one.

℞ HOARD UNCOVERED

An elderly Japanese businessman lost $4 million in cash when a thief found it buried in his garden.

℞ GUILTY CONSCIENCE

A man who robbed a Walnut Creek, California, bank in July 2009 apparently felt so guilty that three days later he walked into a church, confessed to the crime, and handed over $1,200 to a priest before leaving.

℞ WAYWARD SHOT

History buff William Maser, whose hobby is re-creating 19th-century military firearms, accidentally fired a 2-lb (1-kg) cannonball through the wall of his neighbor's home in Georges Township, Pennsylvania, in September 2009. He fired the cannonball, about 2 in (5 cm) in diameter, outside his own home, but it ricocheted and hit a house 400 yd (365 m) away, smashing through a window and a wall before landing in a closet.

HAIR SCULPTURE

CHINESE HAIRDRESSER HUANG XIN SPENT SEVEN DAYS AND NIGHTS CREATING THIS SCULPTURE OF BARACK OBAMA FROM 9 LB (4 KG) OF HUMAN HAIR COLLECTED IN HIS SHOPS. AFTER WASHING AND DYEING THE HAIR—HE USED ONLY WOMEN'S HAIR BECAUSE IT WAS SOFTER—HE GLUED IT ON TO PAPER BEFORE ROLLING IT INTO DIFFERENT SHAPES. HUANG XIN HAS ALSO CREATED A DETAILED MODEL OF BEIJING'S TIANANMEN GATE TOWER FROM HAIR.

Ram Raid

A ram in Helgoysund, Norway, was stranded 15 ft (4.5 m) up a telegraph pole for an hour after it tried to abseil down an electricity cable to reach a field of ewes. The lovelorn sheep slid down the cable from a higher field with his horn stuck on the wire, before stopping against the pole. Eventually a group of German tourists managed to loop a rope around the sheep and lower it to the ground.

℞ ELDERLY GRADUATE

Eleanor Benz, who dropped out of high school to help her family during the Great Depression, finally received her diploma in 2009—73 years later. She left Chicago's Lake View High School at age 17 to take a job, but at her 90th birthday party she was presented with the diploma, gown, and cap, complete with a 1936 tassel.

℞ CARDBOARD CUTOUTS

Flat daddies and flat mommies, life-size cardboard cutout photos of U.S. soldiers stationed abroad, are used to connect families with absent spouses and parents.

℞ EXPLODING FRIDGE

Kathy Cullingworth of West Yorkshire, England, was woken with a start one night when her fridge suddenly exploded. She found the fridge doors had been blown off, scattering food all over the kitchen.

℞ BOTTLE VOYAGE

A message in a bottle dropped off a cruise ship by a U.S. teenager in the Bahamas in 2004 was found five years later on a beach in Cornwall, England—4,000 mi (6,440 km) away. The message had been written by Daniel Knopp of Baltimore, Maryland.

Family Likeness

Dhanna Ram of Rajasthan, India, has been growing his mustache since 1988—and by 2009 it measured 4½ ft (1.4 m) long. He was inspired by the death of his father, Karna Ram Bheel, who himself had a mustache that measured a whopping 6½ ft (2 m) long!

SHARK ATTACK

CRAIG CLASEN FROM MISSISSIPPI FOUGHT A TIGER SHARK FOR OVER TWO HOURS IN A FEROCIOUS BATTLE OF LIFE OR DEATH. CRAIG, AN EXPERT SPEAR FISHERMAN, WAS HUNTING BLUEFIN TUNA IN THE GULF OF MEXICO WITH A SMALL GROUP WHEN A 12-FT (4-M) SHARK BEGAN CIRCLING ONE OF THEM. CRAIG INSTINCTIVELY GRABBED HIS SPEARGUN AND STABBED THE SHARK WHEN IT MADE A MOVE TO ATTACK. ONCE HE HAD INJURED THE CREATURE, CRAIG SAID HE FELT A MORAL OBLIGATION TO FINISH THE JOB AND KILL THE SHARK AS HUMANELY AS POSSIBLE. HE SHOT IT SIX TIMES IN THE HEAD WITH HIS SPEARS, BUT SHARKS ARE EXTREMELY RESILIENT AND HE WAS EVENTUALLY FORCED TO KILL IT WITH A BLADE KNIFE THROUGH ITS SKULL. AN EXPERIENCED DIVER AND FISHERMAN, CRAIG HAS COME INTO CONTACT WITH THOUSANDS OF SHARKS IN HIS LIFETIME AND SAID THAT THIS ENCOUNTER WAS RARE AND THE FIRST INCIDENT WHERE HE HAS HAD TO TAKE SERIOUS ACTION TO PROTECT HIMSELF.

R HOT RIDER

In summer temperatures of up to 118°F (48°C), Omar Al Mamari, founder President of the Oman Bike Club, rode a motorcycle 1,281 mi (2,062 km)—from Muscat to Salalah and back—in 24 hours in 2009.

R FIRE WALL

In March 2009, the Marine Corps Air Station in Yuma, Arizona, created a 15-story-high wall of flame that stretched for 10,173 ft (3,100 m)—that's nearly 2 mi (3.2 km) long. The wall of fire was made up of dynamite, electric blasting caps, and 20,000 ft (6,100 m) of detonation cord.

R DAPPER DAREDEVIL

Dressed in a tweed jacket, and shirt and tie, dapper daredevil Les Pugh of Gloucestershire, England, abseiled down the side of a 160-ft-high (49-m) office block in the town of Cheltenham in April 2009—at age 93!

R ON THE EDGE

In April 2009, 15-year-old Duncan Harris of Normal, Illinois, rode a unicycle on a treacherous 12-mi (19-km) journey along cliff trails at Moab, Utah. He had no brakes except his own legs, no handlebars, and drops of hundreds of feet were just inches away.

R SPEEDY WHEELIE

Fifteen-year-old Jake Drummond maintained a bicycle wheelie for over 330 ft (100 m) at Oshkosh, Wisconsin, in July 2009—and covered the distance in just over 15 seconds.

R DEATH RACE

Among the competitors in the 2009 Canadian Death Race—run over 78 mi (125 km) of mountainous terrain—was a blind woman, 57-year-old Lorraine Pitt from Peterborough, Ontario. Competitors carry their own supplies in the event, held annually in Grand Cache, Alberta. The race begins and ends on a 4,200-ft-high (1,280-m) plateau, passes over three mountain summits as well as bogs, forests, and a river, and includes 17,000 ft (5,180 m) of elevation change.

Mountain Bike

Extreme yoga artist Khiv Raj Gurjar from Jodhpur in Rajasthan, India, balances in extraordinary positions on his bicycle just inches from the edge of rocky outcrops 300 ft (90 m) high. Khiv, who has been practicing and studying yoga since the age of 13, decided to combine both his loves—cycling and yoga—to create this striking discipline in 2006. Now in his sixties, Khiv practices daily for an hour and can perform up to 36 yoga moves balancing on his BMX bike.

R SOLO VOYAGE

Sarah Outen from Rutland, England, rowed solo across the Indian Ocean in 2009, making the 4,000-mi (6,400-km) journey from Perth, Australia, to the island of Mauritius, off the east coast of Africa, in 124 days. She spent up to 12 hours a day rowing, often in scorching sun and riding 30-ft (9-m) waves.

℞ BAR TURNS

In Yerevan, Armenia, in July 2009, Armenian gymnast Davit Fahradyan completed no fewer than 354 turns on a horizontal bar.

℞ LIMBO SKATER

In July 2009, seven-year-old Abbishek Navale, of Belgaum, India, limbo skated backward under ten multi-utility vehicles (Tata Sumo Jeeps). A few days later, he limbo skated backward a distance of 62 ft (18.8 m), under a series of bars positioned just 8.7 in (22 cm) above the ground. Abbishek, who has also skated 335 mi (540 km) from Bangalore to Belgaum in six days, practices his considerable skills for 2½ hours every day.

℞ CANADA RIDE

Riding about 185 mi (300 km) a day, Corneliu Dobrin of Abbotsford, British Columbia, Canada, cycled 4,475 mi (7,200 km) across Canada in just 24 days in July 2009. He departed from Vancouver and finished his epic ride in St. John's, Newfoundland.

℞ KAYAK PLUNGE

Kayaker Tyler Bradt of Missoula, Montana, plunged 186 ft (57 m) in four seconds over the Palouse Falls, Washington State, in July 2009—and emerged with nothing worse than a sprained wrist and a broken paddle. He had visited the spot four times before plucking up the courage to tackle the waterfall, which is so high the spray it generates creates its own rainbow.

℞ BALANCING ACT

Wearing no harness despite being hundreds of feet up in the air, 24-year-old tightrope walker Samat Hasan, from the Xinjiang region of China, climbed 2,300 ft (700 m) along a high wire spanning a valley in Hunan Province in April 2009. The cable was just 1.2 in (3 cm) wide and had a steep gradient of 39 degrees.

℞ YOUNG HUNTER

In September 2009, 16-year-old Cammie Colin of Pelion, South Carolina, bagged an alligator 10 ft 5 in (3.2 m) long and weighing 353 lb (160 kg)—in the middle of the night—with a crossbow. Having won a lottery slot for the state's annual public alligator harvest, she shot her prize while out with her family and a guide in an 18-ft (5.4-m) boat on Lake Marion.

℞ 80 PLUS

Two teams of hockey players—all over the age of 80—took to the ice for a seniors' tournament in Burnaby, British Columbia, Canada in 2009. The oldest player to take part was 87-year-old goaltender Jim Martin.

℞ FINGER POWER

Kung-fu master Ho Eng Hui pierced four coconuts with just his index finger in a little over 30 seconds in Malacca, Malaysia, in June 2009.

℞ COURAGEOUS WALK

Phil Packer, a Royal Military Police Officer in the British Army, was so badly injured in a rocket attack in Basra, Iraq, in February 2008 that he was told he would never walk again. Yet a year later he walked the 26.2-mi (42-km) London Marathon on crutches.

℞ PAPER PLANE

Engineer Takuo Toda, chairman of the Japan Origami Airplane Association, kept a 4-in (10-cm) paper airplane in flight for 27.9 seconds at a competition in Hiroshima Prefecture in April 2009.

℞ BOTTLE BALANCE

In 2008, Alexander Bendikov of Belarus balanced 18,000 matchsticks horizontally on a bottleneck without using any adhesive.

Dirt Diving

On Pentecost Island in the South Pacific, young men prove their courage by making a 75-ft (25-m) bungee jump headfirst into the earth below. The ritual, known as Naghol (land diving), involves up to 25 men a day jumping from a rickety wooden tower with only vines tying their feet together. Traditionally, between the months of April and May, people would jump to bless the soil for an excellent yam harvest. However, today the ritual is a death-defying act of bravery for young men and boys, some as young as seven or eight years old. Elders tie a vine to each foot while women dance and chant at the sides, hoping the men survive.

MAORI MUMMIES

MAORI TRIBES OF NEW ZEALAND USED TO MUMMIFY HEAVILY TATTOOED HEADS OF WARRIOR ADVERSARIES, SKIN, HAIR, TEETH AND ALL. MAORI WARRIORS WOULD COLLECT AS TROPHIES THE DECAPITATED, TATTOOED HEADS OF NOTABLE ENEMIES THEY HAD KILLED IN BATTLE, AND THE HEADS OF THEIR OWN DEAD LEADERS AND FAMILY MEMBERS WERE ALSO REMOVED AND TREATED WITH RESPECT—SOMETIMES TO PREVENT OTHER TRIBES ESCAPING WITH THEM. IT HAS BEEN REPORTED THAT ENTIRE BODIES WERE PRESERVED, ALTHOUGH NONE REMAIN. MAORI FACIAL TATTOOS, KNOWN AS *TA MOKO*, WERE A LONG AND PAINFUL PROCESS, WHICH MADE USE OF CARVED BONE CHISELS TO MAKE CUTS IN THE FACE. IN THE 18TH CENTURY, EUROPEAN VISITORS BEGAN TO BUY THE SKULLS AS INTERESTING ARTIFACTS, AND SOON THE TRADE IN MUMMIFIED *TA MOKO* BECAME SO POPULAR THAT APPROPRIATELY TATTOOED ENEMIES WERE KILLED SOLELY IN ORDER TO SUPPLY THE MARKET WITH FRESH HEADS. THIS MURDEROUS PRACTICE WAS EVENTUALLY OUTLAWED IN THE 19TH CENTURY.

ⓡIPLEY'S RESEARCH

IN ORDER TO MUMMIFY A HEAD, THE MAORIS WOULD FIRST REMOVE THE BRAIN AND THE EYES FROM THE DECAPITATED HEAD. THEN THE EMPTY SKULL AND EYE SOCKETS WERE STUFFED WITH PLANT FIBERS. THE HEAD WAS THEN DRIED OVER A PERIOD OF 24 HOURS USING BOILING, STEAMING, AND SMOKING METHODS.

℞ MODERN CANNIBALS

The journalist Paul Raffaele reported in 2006 that he had discovered a modern headhunter tribe on the island of New Guinea that still removed the heads of their enemies and cannibalized their remains, and they have the skulls to prove it.

℞ DEATH EATERS

The ancient Greek historian Herodotus wrote of a nomadic tribe in Iran that killed and ate members of their community when they became old and weak, cooking them with their cattle. According to his writings, this was the way that they preferred to go.

℞ FROZEN MUMMY

In 1995, two climbers in the Andes discovered the mummified body of a young girl, frozen solid on the side of Mount Ampato. Although it is thought she died in the 15th century, her body was remarkably well preserved.

It is not just heads that could be shrunk. The Jivaros once captured a gold-seeking Spanish army officer and reduced his entire body from a height of 5 ft 9 in (1.75 m) to a shrunken mummy just 31 in (0.78 m) tall.

Robert Ripley holds up a shrunken head from the Jivaro tribes of South America.

℞ UNBURIED HEADS

Headhunting rituals took place in Europe well into the 20th century. Tribes in Montenegro would remove the heads of people they had killed to prevent them receiving a proper burial.

℞ BLUE DOTS

Headhunters of Borneo would mark one finger joint with a blue dot for each victim they had killed. Chief Temonggong Koh had completely blue hands by the time of his death in the late 20th century.

℞ TROPHY BODIES

The Sausa tribe from Peru would skin their enemies, before filling the skin with ash, sewing it back up, and displaying the stuffed skin as a trophy and status symbol.

Head Shrinkers

Some of the most unbelievable discoveries that Robert Ripley made on his travels were the shrunken heads of South America. The Jivaro tribes of Ecuador and Peru would take the heads of fallen enemies, remove the skin whole, and shrink it to the size of a fist. *Tsantas*, as the shrunken heads were known locally, were used to banish the vengeful spirits of their previous owners, with their lips sewn shut to stop the spirits from escaping. When Western tourists began to visit the area in the 19th and 20th centuries, a demand for gruesome souvenirs fueled the practice, and it is said that people were killed just to keep up the supply. Robert Ripley reported in his journal that a German scientist who attempted to find Jivaro headhunters came out of the forest as nothing more than a shrunken head with a red beard. A TV documentary team recently unearthed a Polish videotape from the early 1960s that not only seemed to prove that *tsantas* were still being made by the Jivaro tribe at that time, but also provides remarkable video footage of the head-shrinking process.

℞ GOOD LUCK HEADS

The feared Wa tribe from the jungles of Burma (Myanmar) would regularly cut off people's heads, and did so up until the 1970s, as they thought the severed heads prevented disease and brought good luck.

℞IPLEY'S RESEARCH

THE JIVARO USED TO TAKE A DECAPITATED HEAD AND MAKE AN INCISION IN THE BACK OF THE SCALP SO THAT THEY COULD SLICE THE SKIN, FLESH, AND HAIR OFF THE BONE, MAKING SURE IT REMAINED INTACT. THEN THEY WOULD TAKE THE BONELESS HEAD, SEW THE EYELIDS SHUT, AND SEAL THE MOUTH WITH WOODEN PEGS. THE NEXT PART OF THE PROCESS INVOLVED BOILING THE HEAD FOR NO LESS THAN TWO HOURS IN HERBS THAT CONTAINED TANNIN TO DRY OUT THE HEAD. ONCE REMOVED FROM THE BOIL, THE FLESH WAS SCRAPED FROM THE SKIN AND THE HEAD WAS SHRUNK FURTHER WITH HOT ROCKS AND SAND, BEFORE BEING GRADUALLY MOLDED BACK INTO ITS ORIGINAL SHAPE. FINALLY, THE MOUTH WAS SEWN SHUT WITH STRING AND THE HEAD DRIED OVER A FIRE FOR SEVERAL DAYS.

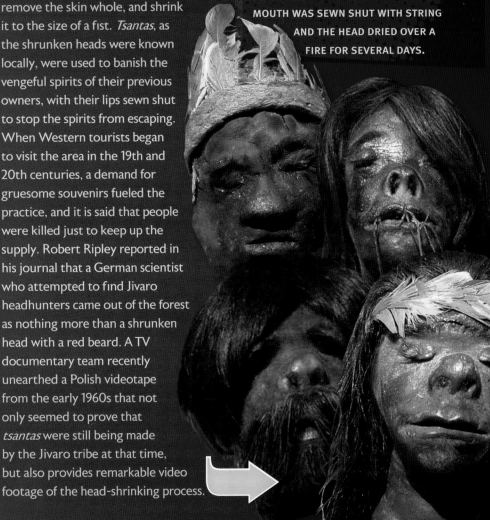

LIGHT SHOW

Thousands of people saw a mysterious giant spiral of light appear in the sky over Norway on the morning of December 9, 2009. It began as a spinning circle of white light centered around a bright moonlike star and then spread out, sending a blue-green beam down to Earth. The eerie phenomenon, which was visible for hundreds of miles, was in the sky for several minutes. Theories included it being a misfired Russian missile, a meteor fireball, or a previously unseen variation of *aurora borealis*, the northern lights.

® STRANGE FOOTPRINTS

Members of a British expedition climbing the north face of Mount Everest in the Himalayas in 1921 spotted a group of dark figures moving around on a snowfield above them. When the climbers reached the spot—at around 21,000 ft (6,400 m)—there was no sign of the creatures; instead, there were huge, humanlike footprints in the snow. Local sherpas said they were the tracks of the elusive Abominable Snowman, or Yeti.

® MISTAKEN IDENTITY

Assistants at a convenience store in Waterloo, Ohio, that had been robbed twice in two months mistook a drunken customer for a robber and threw a bag of cash at him. The man ignored the money and staggered out of the store.

® SCORPION HOME

Suang Puangsri has given up the bottom floor of his two-story home in Thailand to more than 4,600 pet scorpions. A practicing Buddhist, he spends an hour every day meditating inside their enclosure, often placing scorpions in his mouth. He says he has been stung so many times that he has become immune to their venom.

® LAKE WORTH MONSTER

On November 5, 1969, a 7-ft-tall (2.1-m) biped covered in short white fur, with a white goatlike beard, was spotted by many witnesses around Lake Worth, Texas. When someone tried to approach it, the beast howled, threw a car tire some 500 ft (150 m) at the crowd, and fled. Although people discovered footprints 16 in (40-cm) long, no one ever found the Lake Worth Monster.

® ANGRY JEDI

The founder of the Jedi religion inspired by *Star Wars* threatened legal action after he was asked to leave a supermarket for wearing the sect's traditional hood. Daniel Jones from Holyhead, North Wales, leader of the International Church of Jediism, claimed the supermarket victimized him for his beliefs.

® DECAPITATED DUKE

In 1851, builders working in a church near the Tower of London in London, England, discovered a severed head in the vaults. It was discovered to be the Duke of Suffolk, an aristocrat decapitated at the Tower in 1554, his head well preserved by sawdust from the scaffolding on which he lost his head.

® LAWN RANGER

Stan Hardwick of North Yorkshire, England, owns a lawn mower for every day of the year. Known as the Lawn Ranger, he has spent thousands of dollars on over 365 mowers, some dating back to the mid-19th century. He keeps his favorites in the house for visitors to admire, and stores the rest in his garden shed.

® SKULL RIDDLE

A yellowing skull uncovered near Featherston on New Zealand's North Island in 2004 was identified by forensic pathologists as having belonged to a European woman who lived around 270 years ago—a century before the first known arrival of white settlers in the country.

® JELLYFISH ASSULT

In September 2009, a 41-year-old man was arrested on Madeira Beach, Florida, accused of throwing jellyfish at teenagers.

® DEATH ROAD

In the first 12 months after a new section of highway opened between the German towns of Bremen and Bremerhaven in 1929, there were over 100 crashes close to a small roadside kilometer marker known as marker 239—even though the section of road was straight and flat. On one clear day in September 1930, nine cars left the road here. A local man said an underground stream was generating a strong magnetic current that caused the crashes, so he buried a copper-filled copper box there, after which the accidents stopped.

® CHIMP CANDIDATE

A bad-tempered chimpanzee that had a habit of throwing excrement at visitors to Brazil's Rio de Janeiro Zoo was nominated by a satirical magazine to run for the city's 1988 mayoral election. Tiao polled more than 400,000 votes, finishing third out of the 12 candidates.

®IPLEY'S RESEARCH

THE LEGEND OF THE YETI DATES BACK TO 1832 WHEN HIMALAYAN GUIDES SPOTTED A TALL, DARK, HAIRY CREATURE WALKING UPRIGHT ON TWO LEGS LIKE A HUMAN. SINCE THEN, THERE HAVE BEEN NUMEROUS EXPEDITIONS IN SEARCH OF THE YETI (OR ABOMINABLE SNOWMAN). HOWEVER, ALTHOUGH THERE HAVE BEEN OCCASIONAL SIGHTINGS, AND STRANGE FOOTPRINTS HAVE BEEN DISCOVERED IN THE SNOW, THE BEAST'S TRUE IDENTITY HAS NEVER BEEN REVEALED. EXPERTS HAVE SUGGESTED IT COULD BE AN ORANGUTAN, A BEAR, A LANGUR MONKEY, OR, MOST INTRIGUINGLY, AN UNKNOWN SPECIES.

Legend of the Yeti

U.S. TV-show host Josh Gates displays a cast of what may be footprints of the elusive Yeti, an apelike creature whose existence has been shrouded in mystery for nearly 200 years. The tracks—measuring about 13 in (33 cm) long—were found in 2007 at an altitude of 9,350 ft (2,850 m) near Mount Everest in Nepal.

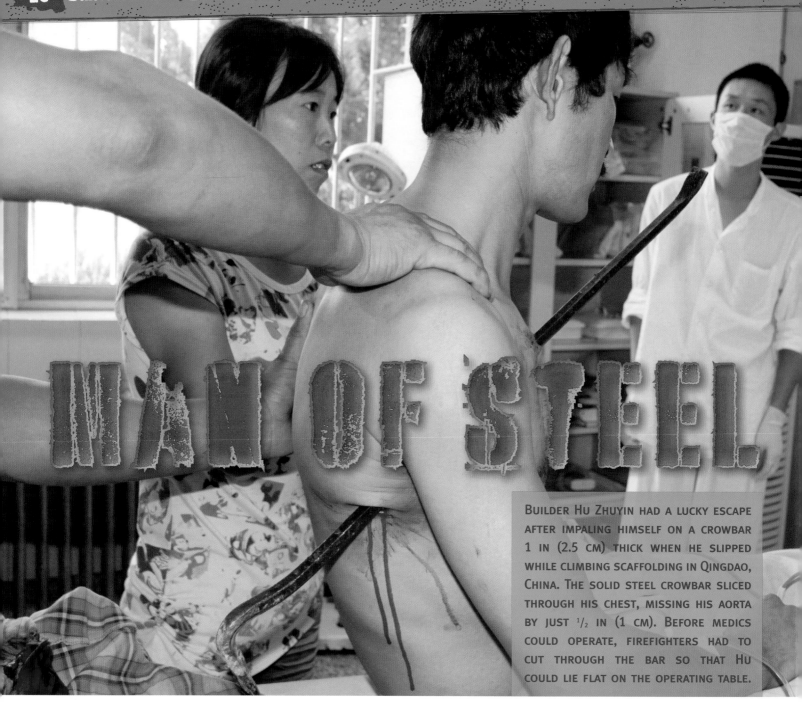

MAN OF STEEL

BUILDER HU ZHUYIN HAD A LUCKY ESCAPE AFTER IMPALING HIMSELF ON A CROWBAR 1 IN (2.5 CM) THICK WHEN HE SLIPPED WHILE CLIMBING SCAFFOLDING IN QINGDAO, CHINA. THE SOLID STEEL CROWBAR SLICED THROUGH HIS CHEST, MISSING HIS AORTA BY JUST $^1/_2$ IN (1 CM). BEFORE MEDICS COULD OPERATE, FIREFIGHTERS HAD TO CUT THROUGH THE BAR SO THAT HU COULD LIE FLAT ON THE OPERATING TABLE.

℞ LODGED IN BRAIN

A large metal pin broke off and lodged itself in the brain of 19-year-old Chris Clear from Penrose, Colorado, while he was helping a friend move a rototiller. Luckily, the pin narrowly missed several major arteries and, after a nine-hour operation to remove it, Clear was able to return to work as a volunteer firefighter. There is not even a scar to remind him of the accident, but he kept the pin as a souvenir.

℞ BROKEN LEG

After suffering decades of pain, Steve Webb from Essex, England, discovered he had been walking around with a broken leg for 29 years. He broke his left leg in a motorbike crash when he was 20 and in 2009 found that it had never actually healed.

℞ ALL'S WELL

An 84-year-old man survived with only minor injuries after spending four days trapped in a well in June 2009. Bob Bennett had entered the 8-ft-deep (2.4-m) well shaft on his remote property at Benson Lake, British Columbia, Canada, while searching for a water source.

℞ HIDDEN PAIN

In April 2009, doctors treated Mrike Rrucaj of Albania for severe head pain and found a bullet that had been lodged in her cheek for 12 years without her knowing it.

℞ ELDERLY MOM

In November 2008, Rajo Devi from the state of Haryana, India, gave birth to a healthy baby at 70 years of age.

℞ CONCEALED WEAPON

Despite being searched several times, obese 540-lb (255-kg) George Vera was able to smuggle a gun into two different Texas jails by hiding it within his rolls of fat.

℞ NEW SKULL

A man whose skull was partially removed after an accident over 50 years ago has stunned doctors by growing a new one— something that is thought to have happened only once before. Gordon Moore of Northumberland, England, had worn a metal plate for half a century after being involved in a car crash, but when surgeons removed the plate in 2009 to treat an infection, they were amazed to find he had grown a completely new skull underneath.

℞ UTENSIL REMOVED

Doctors puzzled by the coughing fits that plagued a man for almost two years found the answer in 2009 by removing a 1-in (2.5-cm) fragment of a plastic eating utensil from his lung. John Manley of Wilmington, North Carolina, said he probably inhaled the piece of plastic while gulping a drink at a fast-food restaurant.

℞ MAGGOT INFESTATION

After suffering from constant nosebleeds for five days, a 70-year-old woman had 40 maggots removed from her nose by doctors at a hospital in Sion, India. A housefly had entered her nose and laid eggs inside it. When the eggs hatched, the larvae started feeding on her flesh, causing her nose to bleed.

℞ STRETCHED LEGS

In an attempt to be taken more seriously at work, Hajnal Ban, a politician from Logan, Queensland, Australia, paid a Russian surgeon $30,000 to break her legs and stretch them so that she would be 5 ft 4 in (1.62 m) tall, three inches taller than her original height.

℞ TEARS OF BLOOD

Teenager Calvino Inman of Rockwood, Tennessee, has a medical condition that leads to him crying tears of blood. The bleeding, which can last for up to an hour, occurs at least three times a day.

Swallowed Scissors

A man in Putian, China, accidentally swallowed a pair of scissors 3½ in (9 cm) long and 1½ in (4 cm) wide. Mr. Lin was using the scissors as a toothpick but when he suddenly laughed, they slipped down into his throat. He tried unsuccessfully to cough them back up and the scissors eventually had to be removed by surgery.

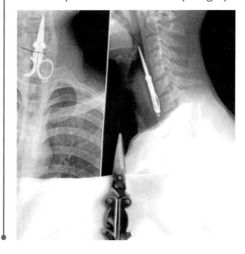

℞ AIRPLANE DEBRIS

Wissam Beydoun of Dearborn, Michigan, was standing outside his home talking in 2009 when he was hit on the shoulder by a piece of metal that had fallen from an airplane. The aluminum scrap, which measured 8 x 6 in (20 x 15 cm) and weighed about a quarter of an ounce, left him with nothing worse than a bump.

Giant Grave

After 990-lb (450-kg) José Luis Garza died in Juarez, Mexico, in 2008, carpenters built him a special extra-large coffin, which had to be lowered into a massive grave by 20 people.

℞ PARROT TALK

A U.S. firefighter who lost his power of speech in a road accident in 1995 has been taught to speak again by parrots. Brian Wilson from Damascus, Maryland, suffered such a serious head injury that doctors told him he would probably never be able to speak coherently again. However, two of the pet parrots that he had kept since childhood continually talked to him, and eventually he began to respond. To show his gratitude, he now provides a home for around 80 abandoned or unwanted parrots.

℞ SECOND BABY

Julia Grovenburg of Fort Smith, Arkansas, stunned doctors by conceiving for a second time while already pregnant. When Mrs. Grovenburg went for her first ultrasound scan, she thought she was about eight weeks pregnant—and she was, with a baby boy. However, she was also almost 11 weeks pregnant with a baby girl, who was developing next to her younger brother in their mother's womb. The non-twins are thought to represent an extremely rare case of superfetation.

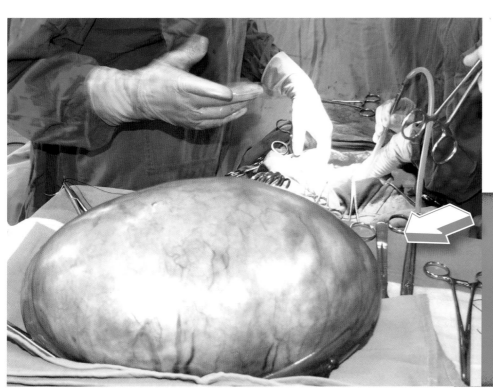

Sumo Cyst

A Chinese woman thought she was pregnant with her first child, only to find that she was instead carrying an ovarian cyst weighing 7 lb 11 oz (3.5 kg). Surgeons at a hospital in Haikou successfully removed the cyst—the largest ovarian cyst found in over 20 years.

Wooly Wedding

Shepherdess Louise Fairburn from Lincolnshire, England, got married in a wedding dress made of wool from one of her own flock. Husband Ian wore a woolen waistcoat made from the same sheep. The dress took 120 hours to make and cost around £3,000. Louise, who even carried a Bo Peep-style crook on her big day, loves her sheep so much that they featured in her wedding photos.

℞ SAME NAME

Kelly Hildebrandt, a student from Miami, Florida, announced her engagement in 2009 to... Kelly Hildebrandt. Bored one evening, she had entered her name on the social networking website Facebook to see what would appear and found one match—a Kelly Hildebrandt from Lubbock, Texas. She sent him a message, they became friends and after visiting her in Florida, he proposed.

℞ TEXT DOCTOR

Caroline Tagg, a postgraduate academic at Birmingham University, England, has been awarded a doctorate in text messaging. She spent 3¹/₂ years writing an 80,000-word thesis on SMS texts and their language after studying more than 11,000 texts (that contained a total of around 190,000 words) sent by friends.

℞ MARATHON MARRIAGE

Rachel Pitt and Garry Keates of Hertfordshire, England, got married while running the 2009 London marathon. They took a detour 24 mi (38.6 km) into the race to jog down the aisle of St. Bride's church, on Fleet Street. Still wearing running shoes, they later completed the remaining 2¹/₄ mi (3.5 km) hand-in-hand before the groom carried his new bride over the finish line as she threw her bouquet into the crowd.

℞ DOUBLE EGG

Farmer Jeff Taylor from Herefordshire, England, got the shock of his life when he found an egg inside another egg! Both eggs were intact and perfectly formed. Double eggs are thought to be the result of some malfunction in the hen's rhythmic muscular action, which moves a developing egg down the oviduct.

Musical Heights

In 2008, extreme cellists set themselves a 48-hour time limit to climb the four highest mountains in Britain and Ireland with cellos, perform a concert, and cover the 1,000 mi (1,600 km) between the peaks. The challenge, completed successfully, followed performances in or on the roofs of 42 British cathedrals—a feat that they managed in just 12 days—and a concert at every street on the London Monopoly board in a day.

LIGHT SNACK

A CUBAN TREE FROG THAT TRIED TO CATCH AN INSECT IN A PALM BEACH, FLORIDA, GARDEN ENDED UP GLOWING IN THE DARK AFTER SWALLOWING A FAIRY LIGHT. THE BUG HAD LANDED ON THE COLORED LIGHT IN WILDLIFE PHOTOGRAPHER JAMES SNYDER'S GARDEN, BUT WHEN THE FROG WENT IN FOR THE KILL, IT SWALLOWED THE ENTIRE BULB, TOO.

℞ ICING ON THE CAKE

When Neil Berrett of San Francisco, California, decided to quit his job at a naval shipyard in 2009, he had his letter of resignation written in icing on top of a cake.

℞ ZERO GRAVITY

A couple from Brooklyn, New York, proved they were head over heels in love during their wedding by getting married in zero gravity. Science fiction fans Noah Fulmor and Erin Finnegan paid over $15,000 to have their wedding at Kennedy Space Center in a converted Boeing 727 jet airplane which, in the course of a special 90-minute flight, undertakes spectacular roller-coaster-style dives, which simulates the weightlessness experienced by astronauts on space walks. As they floated on air, the couple exchanged rings made from precious metal fragments of a meteorite that crashed to Earth in Namibia 30,000 years ago.

℞ FALLING FISH

Leighann Niles was driving near Marblehead, Ohio, in August 2009 when her car windshield was smashed by a falling fish dropped from the talons of an eagle. She said the impact of the fish—a Lake Erie freshwater drum—felt like a brick hitting her car.

℞ MAKING HAY

A farmer's son, Markus Schmidt, spelt out his marriage proposal to girlfriend Corinna Pesl by rolling 150 bales of hay to form the words "Will you marry me?" Each bale of hay weighed 661 lb (300 kg) and each letter was 11½ ft (3.5 m) high. Corinna saw the 227-ft-long (70-m) message when she looked out of the bedroom window of her home in the Upper Bavaria region of Germany.

℞ PARKING TICKET

A traffic warden in Darwin, Northern Territory, Australia, gave a dog a parking ticket after it was left outside a shopping market. An elderly lady left the dog tied to a fence outside the Rapid Creek market while she went shopping, but when she returned she found that an inspector had attached a ticket to the dog's leash.

℞ WEDDING RUSH

Tens of thousands of Chinese people rushed to get married on September 9, 2009, believing that the 09/09/09 date was a good omen for a long marriage. The ninth day of the ninth month, "*jiu, jiu*" in Chinese, is a homonym for "*jiujiu,*" which means "for a very long time."

BODY SNATCHERS

WELCOME TO THE WORLD OF THE PARASITE, AND WHAT A WORLD IT IS! THESE GUYS ARE FRIGHTENINGLY SMART—THEY LIVE ON, OR IN, ANOTHER ORGANISM AND MANIPULATE THE BEHAVIOR OF THEIR UNSUSPECTING HOSTS TO THEIR ADVANTAGE, OFTEN KILLING THEM IN THE PROCESS.

Deadly Mushroom

Spores invade, insect dies, fungi grows out of corpse

These fungi infect caterpillars and other insects, killing them and mummifying the body as they spread. Some fungi make insects into zombies, whereby the insects crawl along and die in the best place for the fungi spores to spread into the air and infect other insects.

Brain Eaters

Fly drops larva that will eat ant's brain until its head falls off

The fly lands on the head of an ant, laying an egg that releases a brain-eating larva. The larva eventually decapitates the ant and lives in the head for two weeks until it emerges as an adult Phorid fly.

This parasite invades snails, making their eyestalks swollen and colorful to encourage birds, which then attack the snails and rip off their eyestalks. The flatworms breed in the birds' guts. Other snails then eat bird droppings infected with the parasite, and the endless cycle continues.

Stuck for Life

Male fish fuse with females for life!

Male anglerfish are much smaller than female anglerfish. They bite onto the body of females until their skin and eventually their blood vessels fuse together. The withered male then becomes part of the female body forever, useless except for his role in fertilizing the female's eggs.

Eye Catching

Infected snail eyestalks look like pulsating green caterpillars

Mind Control

Hairworms begin life as tiny creatures living in the guts of insects, which they start eating from the inside until they grow to be longer than their hosts—up to 3 ft (1 m) in length! The presence of the worm drives the insect to seek out water, where it drowns. The adult worm then squeezes itself out of its host and lives in the water.

Makes insects drown themselves so water-dwelling worm can escape into water

Womb Invader

Parasite takes over crab egg pouch

A parasitic barnacle attaches itself to crabs, invades the egg pouch, and forces the crab to look after parasite eggs. If the crab is male, the parasite sterilizes it and makes its abdomen bigger, essentially turning the male crab female.

Hunter Hunted

Paralyzes tarantula so young wasp can eat it

Tarantula hawk wasps hunt tarantulas and paralyze them with a powerful sting—one of the most painful ever recorded. The spider is dragged back to its own nest, where the wasp lays an egg on its body. When the wasp larva hatches, the paralyzed spider is eaten alive.

Replaces fish tongue to feed on blood and mucus

Taste Buddy

This creature clamps onto the tongue of a fish, sucking blood from the tongue until it withers and dies. The parasite then remains firmly attached in the fish's mouth, working just like the original tongue, but dining on blood, mucus, and scraps of food.

℞ CHAMPION CRAWLER

The city of Vilnius, Lithuania, stages an annual baby-crawling contest where tiny tots crawl along a 16-ft (5-m) carpeted track, encouraged by their parents waving keys and toys at the finish line. The 2009 winner was eight-month-old Kajus Aukscionis, who completed the course in 18 seconds.

Claws Encounter

INSPIRED BY EDWARD SCISSORHANDS, VALENTINO LOSAURO HAS DEVELOPED FINGERTIP SCISSORS, WHICH ARE MADE FROM ELASTIC AND RAZOR-SHARP STEEL. THEY CUT HAIR TWICE AS FAST AS SCISSORS, CLAIMS LOSAURO, A PIANIST, WHO WANTED TO APPLY THE LIGHT-FINGER TOUCH OF PIANO PLAYING TO STYLING HAIR. "WHEN I CUT HAIR I USE METHODS I CALL 'FLIGHT OF THE BUMBLEBEE,'" HE SAYS, REFERRING TO THE QUICK-FINGER ACTION HE NOW USES AT HIS FLORIDA SALON. "I CAN'T BELIEVE HOW LONG A CUT USED TO TAKE."

Case in Point

It took George Gaspar, from Sherman Oaks, California, just 90 minutes to insert 2,222 toothpicks into his beard.

℞ KISSING FRENZY

Twenty young women lined up in Blackburn, England, in 2009 to give 28-year-old local DJ Paul Winstanley 110 kisses in one minute— that's almost two kisses a second.

℞ DUCK RACE

A staggering 205,000 plastic ducks floated 0.6 mi (1 km) down the River Thames near London, England, in the 2009 Great British Duck Race.

℞ BRICK SMASHER

Using a combination of speed and power, German martial arts expert Bernd Hoehle smashed 12 freestanding bricks in just eight seconds in Hanover, Germany, in 2009.

℞ MOOSE FAN

Al Goddard of Takoma Park, Maryland, has collected more than 1,000 items of moose memorabilia. His collection began in 1975 when he was teaching at a school in Oakton, Virginia, and a student presented him with a stuffed toy moose as a gift.

℞ COFFIN MAKER

During a career spanning more than 30 years, carpenter Herbert Weber from Austria's Salzburg province has built over 700,000 coffins.

℞ PUMPKIN FACES

In October 2008, Stephen Clarke of Havertown, Pennsylvania, carved jack-o'-lantern faces into one ton's worth of pumpkins in 3 hours 33 minutes 49 seconds at Atlantic City, New Jersey.

ℝ YOUNG PARAGLIDER

Luan Da Silva from Florianopolis, Brazil, is already an experienced paraglider even though he is just six years old. Both of his parents are paragliding instructors and he made his first flight with his father at age two and his first solo flight a year later. Sitting in a specially weighted harness to stop him from blowing away, Luan loves to leap from the top of a sand dune and soar 65 ft (20 m) into the air.

ℝ WEEKLY COLUMN

At age 102, former 1940s pin-up girl Margaret Caldwell was still writing a weekly column, "Memoirs of a Crone," for the *Desert Valley Times* newspaper in Mesquite, Nevada.

ℝ TALKATIVE TEEN

Thirteen-year-old Reina Hardesty from Orange County, California, used her cell phone to send 14,528 text messages during the month of December 2008. That worked out at 484 text messages every day—an average of one message every two minutes while she was awake. The online monthly phone-bill statement ran to 440 pages.

ℝ GIANT PUZZLE

Indian jigsaw-puzzle enthusiasts created an online jigsaw puzzle with 25,000 pieces in 2009. The challenge attracted over 180,000 participants, each working with 1,000 blocks of 25 pieces to assemble a large image designed by New Zealand jigsaw expert Royce B. McClure. In its physical form, the puzzle measured 36 x 16 ft (11 x 5 m).

ℝ ZOMBIE PARTY

In July 2009, a grand total of 3,894 people dressed as zombies for the "Red, White, and Dead Zombie Party" event in Seattle, Washington State.

ℝ FAMILY RUN

Sixteen brothers and sisters from the Kapral family of Oshkosh, Wisconsin, finished the 2009 Fox Cities Marathon— and all in under six hours. Only two of the family—brothers Vince and Stephen—had completed a full marathon before.

ℝ KITE DISPLAY

Some 4,000 Palestinian children flew kites simultaneously for 30 seconds on beaches of the Gaza Strip in July 2009.

ℝ YOSEMITE WALK

Without any safety equipment, American Dean Potter walked an unleashed slackline—a rope length that isn't taut—3,200 ft (960 m) above the floor of Yosemite Valley, California. The only things holding him to the rope during his 100-ft (30-m) walk were his size-14 feet.

ℝ PIE FIGHT

More than 200 people took part in a mass pie fight on a farm at Genoa, Illinois, in 2009. The fight, organized by farm-owner Molly Holbrook, involved participants hurling chocolate, meringue, pumpkin, and custard pies at each other.

ℝ MILK DELIVERY

For nearly 100 years, three generations of the Hall family delivered milk to the village of Gunnislake in Cornwall, England, placing an estimated 20 million pints on people's doorsteps. The last in the line, Jo Hall, retired in 2009 after 55 years in the job, during which time she clocked up 176,000 mi (283,245 km) doing her milk delivery round.

ℝ FLOWER GARLAND

In May 2009, residents of San Pedro, the Philippines, strung together a *sampaguita lei*—a flower garland—that measured more than 1¼ mi (2 km) long.

A Game of Squash

Austrian artist Willi Dorner is causing a stir across Europe by squeezing bodies into nooks and crannies across the continent. Groups of dancers, climbers, and performers, wearing brightly colored clothes, run through busy malls and high streets and suddenly cram themselves into doorways, trees, and any gap they can find.

ON THE BALL

RIPLEY'S LOVED THE GIANT RUBBER-BAND BALL MADE BY JOEL WAUL SO MUCH THAT IT BOUGHT IT. THE PROBLEM WAS GETTING THE GIANT BALL, MADE FROM 780,000 RUBBER BANDS, TO RIPLEY'S ORLANDO WAREHOUSE FOR STORAGE. AT 9,400 LB (4,264 KG) AND 7 FT (2.1 M) TALL, THE BALL IS NOT EASY TO MANEUVER AND CAN BE DANGEROUS— RIPLEY'S PREVIOUSLY REPORTED THAT, WHEN THE BALL WAS JUST 400 LB (181 KG), IT ROLLED OVER AND SPRAINED WAUL'S HAND. IN OCTOBER 2009, A RIPLEY'S TEAM ARRIVED AT WAUL'S LAUDERHILL, FLORIDA, HOME WITH A TRANSPORTER TRUCK AND CRANE. THE BALL WAS CAREFULLY HAULED UP FROM WAUL'S DRIVE (IT SMELLS TOO BAD TO HAVE BEEN KEPT IN HIS HOUSE) AND LOADED ONTO THE TRUCK, BEFORE MAKING A SLOW JOURNEY TO THE WAREHOUSE. ITS PERMANENT HOME WILL BE THE RIPLEY'S MUSEUM IN HOLLYWOOD, CALIFORNIA, WHICH IS TEMPORARILY WITHOUT A ROOF, SO THAT IT CAN BE LOWERED IN. IT IS TOO BIG TO ROLL THROUGH A DOOR, AND ONLY JUST MADE IT INTO THE WAREHOUSE!

RIPLEY REVISITED

Up in Flames

In 2009, 17 people were each completely engulfed in fire without oxygen supplies at the same time in South Russell, Ohio. The group, led by local man Ted Batchelor, walked around Bell Road with their bodies in flames for an amazing 43.9 seconds. The team prepared for eight months for the event in their burn suits, and not one person sustained even a minor injury as the feat took place.

℞ TOILET LINE

In an event organized by the United Nations' children's agency UNICEF to raise awareness for the need for clean water, 756 people lined up to visit a toilet in Brussels, Belgium, in March 2009.

℞ BOOK TOWER

In June 2009, John Evans of Derbyshire, England, balanced 204 books on his head in a pyramid-shaped tower that was 4 ft (1.2 m) high and weighed 284 lb (129 kg). The contents of a can of hairspray were used to stop the books from slipping off his head.

℞ NONAGENARIAN SKYDIVER

In April 2009, George Moyse of Dorset, England, went skydiving for the first time—at age 97. Strapped to an instructor, he jumped out of an airplane at 10,000 ft (3,048 m) above Salisbury Plain, Wiltshire, and carried out a free fall for the first 5,000 ft (1,525 m) at speeds of nearly 120 mph (193 km/h).

℞ HUMAN WHEELBARROWS

In Singapore in April 2009, no fewer than 1,378 students from Temasek Polytechnic took part in a mass human wheelbarrow race. At the same event, students formed an unbroken human wheelbarrow chain comprising 74 people.

In the warehouse!

℞ PAPER BALL

To illustrate the importance of recycling and the enormity of waste, Enrique Miramontes and Ricardo Granados—two friends from San Diego, California—have spent more than six years creating a giant ball of discarded paper that weighs 200 lb (91 kg) and is 3 ft (1 m) high. In that time Miramontes alone has spent over $3,000 on masking tape and over 2,000 hours layering the pieces of paper on top of each other. He had the idea as a 16-year-old high school student when a friend threw a rolled up ball of paper at him in biology class.

℞ MELON SMASH

At the 2009 Chinchilla Melon Festival, held in Queensland, Australia, local melon picker John Allwood smashed 47 watermelons with his head in one minute.

℞ TREE PLANTERS

On a single day in July 2009, a team of 300 volunteers planted more than half a million mangrove trees in the Indus River delta region of Sindh province, in southern Pakistan.

℞ MASS KISS

On Valentine's Day 2009, nearly 40,000 people (20,000 couples) gathered in Mexico City's main square and kissed for 10 seconds.

℞ REVERSE WALK

In 2008, Bill Kathan of Vernon, Vermont, walked backward from one rim of the Grand Canyon, down to the basin, and back up the other side in 15 hours.

℞ YOUNG CLIMBER

Six-year-old Tom Fryers from South Yorkshire, England, has already climbed 214 peaks in England's Lake District—the equivalent of climbing five Mount Everests. Tom scaled his first peak when he was just three and has since covered 480 mi (772 km) and climbed more than 150,000 ft (45,720 m), including the two highest mountains in England— 3,209-ft (978-m) Scafell Pike and 3,162-ft (964-m) Sca Fell.

FEATURELESS FACE

IF VISITORS TO THE CHIESA DELLA SANTA CHURCH IN BOLOGNA, ITALY, GAZE LONG ENOUGH INTO A GRATED OPENING IN THE CHURCH WALL, A STRANGE, DARK, ALMOST FEATURELESS FACE WILL STARE BACK AT THEM. THE SPOOKY APPARITION IS THE MUMMIFIED RELIC OF ST. CATHERINE OF BOLOGNA. SHE DIED IN 1475, BUT AFTER A SERIES OF MIRACLES, HER BODY, INEXPLICABLY SHOWING LITTLE SIGN OF DECAY, WAS EXHUMED BY NUNS. A FEW YEARS LATER, CATHERINE APPEARED TO ONE OF THE NUNS IN A VISION, ASKING TO BE PLACED IN THE SMALL CHAPEL, SITTING UPRIGHT. SO THEY DRESSED HER IN NUN'S CLOTHING, PLACED A GOLDEN CROSS IN HER HAND, AND SAT HER IN A GOLDEN CHAIR, WHERE SHE HAS REMAINED FOR MORE THAN 500 YEARS.

℞ HIDDEN TREASURE

For over 200 years, treasure hunters have tried to get to the bottom of the so-called "money pit" on Oak Island, Nova Scotia, Canada. The 200-ft-deep (60-m) pit was first discovered by Daniel McGinnis in 1795 but flooding, collapse, and a series of booby traps have since made it impenetrable. Six treasure hunters have been killed in the quest, believing the pit to contain a valuable haul of treasure. Theories as to the exact nature of the treasure include it being a pirate's booty, the French crown jewels, the treasures of King Solomon's temple, or even the Holy Grail.

℞ NAZCA LINES

Across a plain 50 mi (80 km) long and 15 mi (24 km) wide on Peru's arid Nazca Desert sit a series of around 900 huge geometric shapes, ranging from simple lines to complex drawings depicting animals, plants, and birds. They include a spider, a hummingbird, a whale, and a 1,000-ft-long (300-m) pelican. One of the straight lines is 9 mi (15 km) long. The forms are so difficult to spot from the ground that they were not discovered until the 1930s when a plane flew over the plateau.

℞ SPRING-HEELED JACK

A seemingly respectable man walked into a London police station in 1837 and recounted how his daughter had been attacked by a cloaked figure who had blue and white flames shooting from his mouth, and metallic claws. Renowned for his ability to leap remarkable heights, the mysterious character known as Spring-Heeled Jack continued to fascinate and terrify Victorian London for years and was even reported as far afield as Liverpool and Scotland.

℞ MARY CELESTE

Built in Nova Scotia, Canada, the 282-ton merchant ship *Mary Celeste* sailed from New York in November 1872 bound for Genoa, Italy, with a cargo of 1,701 barrels of alcohol—yet when it was discovered off Portugal on December 4, the ten people on board had completely vanished and were never heard from again. There was no sign of a struggle, the cargo was largely intact, the ship was in excellent condition, the weather was calm, and the crew were experienced. Although the ship's lifeboat was missing, the belongings of the crew and passengers had all been left onboard.

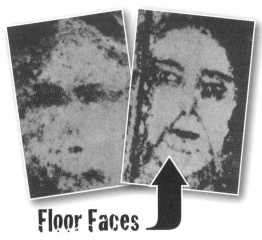

Floor Faces

Maria Gomez Pereira was startled to see an image of a man's face suddenly appear on the kitchen floor of her house in Belmez, Spain, in 1971. She had the floor pulled up and relaid, but the face reappeared in the exact same spot within a week. It was discovered that the house was built on a graveyard, and excavations beneath the floor revealed human remains, which were duly removed. A new floor was then laid, but within two weeks a series of faces began appearing again.

℞ MOUNTAIN LIGHTS

For more than 800 years, mysterious groups of lights have been observed on Brown Mountain, North Carolina. The lights are usually white, but have also been known to turn red, blue, or yellow. One theory is that they are the result of swamp gas released by decaying animal and plant matter, but there are no swamps in the area. Others suggest the illuminations could be ball lightning.

Masked Man

For a century it was believed that in 1908 adventurer Harry Bensley had set off from London on a six-year trek around the world, wearing an iron mask and pushing a pram to win a $100,000 bet with eccentric American millionaire J. Pierpont Morgan. However, far from reaching China and Japan as he had claimed, there is now doubt that Bensley ever left Britain. His family can find no evidence of him venturing abroad, and when he resurfaced he showed no signs of wealth, even though his supposed winnings were the equivalent of over $2 million today. So the mysterious case of Harry Bensley remains unsolved.

℞ WHITE RIVER MONSTER

Fishing on the White River at Newport, Arkansas, in 1971, Cloyce Warren and his friends saw a huge spout of water rise skyward. Moments later a 30-ft-long (9-m) creature with a spiny backbone briefly surfaced before disappearing back into the depths. Although Warren managed to take a photo of it, the White River Monster has never been identified.

℞ STONE STATUES

Nearly 900 giant stone statues, at least 400 years old, with elongated human heads and torsos, are scattered across Easter Island in the South Pacific—but nobody knows why the islanders built them or how they transported them into position. The statues—or *moai*—are an average 13 ft (4 m) high and weigh 14 tons (although some weigh more than 80 tons), and it is estimated that up to 150 people would have been needed to drag each one across the countryside on wooden sleds.

℞ KILLER EAGLE

Research in 2009 showed that a huge man-eating bird of prey from ancient Maori legend really did exist. The Maoris of New Zealand told of a massive bird that would swoop down on people in the mountains and kill children. Scientists have known about a giant eagle for more than a century, based on excavated bones, but new studies of its behavior indicate a truly fearsome predator weighing up to 40 lb (18 kg) that probably did attack humans.

℞ ELTANIN ANTENNA

In 1964, the U.S. polar research vessel *Eltanin* found a strange antenna at the bottom of the Atlantic Ocean, 1,000 mi (1,600 km) south of Cape Horn. It was a pole with 12 spokes radiating from it. The spokes were at an angle of 15 degrees from one another and each had a spherical shape on the end. Some experts thought it was a new marine life form; others believed it to be a relic of an ancient civilization.

Snap!

Conjoined crocodile twins were born at the Samut Prakarn Crocodile Farm and Zoo near Bangkok, Thailand. The animals, named Chang and Eng after the world's most famous Siamese twins (see page 15), each had a head and four legs, but shared a common lower body with one tail.

℞ CASH FIND

While walking to his car in Syracuse, New York, in 2009, David Jenks noticed a number of bags apparently containing trash lying by the side of the street—but when he went to move them he discovered that they were filled with $250,000 in banknotes.

℞ CHILD'S PLAY

Three-year-old Pipi Quinlan from Auckland, New Zealand, visited an online auction site in 2009 and bought a mechanical shovel for $12,000 while her parents were asleep.

℞ WINNING TICKET

Two months after her husband Donald's death, Charlotte Peters of Danbury, Connecticut, checked through his belongings and found a $10 million winning lottery ticket. He had bought the ticket just hours before suffering a fatal heart attack in November 2008.

℞ SNAIL MAIL

In July 2009, Wendy Bosworth from Wolverhampton, West Midlands, England, received a postcard from a Greek island— 22 years after it was sent. The card had been posted by her niece, Joanne Bosworth, who was holidaying on the island of Nisyros in 1987.

Head Drill

Chinese kung fu master Hu Qiong can insert a fast-spinning electric drill into his temple and belly for a full minute and walk away unharmed. Known as "The Unbreakable Body," Hu can also catch a running electric saw with his bare hands.

℞ SNAP DECISION

An anti-Mafia police unit in Naples, Italy, seized a crocodile that was used by an alleged mobster to intimidate local businessmen. Officers said the gangster would invite extortion victims to his home and threaten them with the crocodile, which weighed 88 lb (40 kg) and was 5 ft 7 in (1.7 m) long, unless they paid him protection money.

℞ MISSILE CATCH

Commercial fisherman Rodney Salomon from St. Petersburg, Florida, landed the catch of his life in 2009—an 8-ft-long (2.4-m), American-made, air-to-air guided missile that could have exploded at any moment. Despite the danger, he reeled in the missile, strapped it to the roof of his boat, and kept fishing in the Gulf of Mexico for another ten days—even during electrical storms—before returning to port.

℞ DOUBLE LIFE

Two women who worked at the same factory in Zhengzhou, China, were shocked to learn they were both married to the same man. Cui Bin divided his time between the two households, making excuses for his frequent absences. Meanwhile, the two wives had become friends through a shared love of karaoke, never dreaming that they were also sharing a husband.

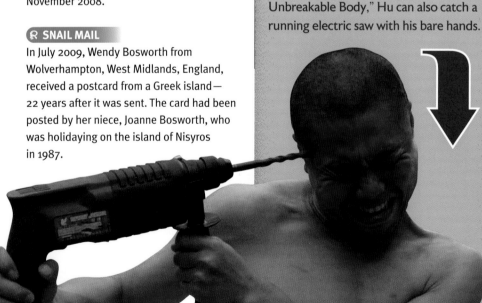